D1807909

Your Child's Baptism

A GUIDE TO THE SERVICE
AND ITS MEANING

David Winter

LION
Giftlines

Published by
Lion Publishing plc
Sandy Lane West, Oxford, England
ISBN 0 7459 3372 6
Albatross Books Pty Ltd
PO Box 320, Sutherland, NSW 2232, Australia
ISBN 0 7324 1334 6

First edition 1995
10 9 8 7 6 5 4 3 2 1 0

Acknowledgments
Text from the Alternative Service Book 1980 is
reproduced by permission of the Central Board of
Finance of the Church of England.

A catalogue record for this book is available
from the British Library

Printed and bound in Great Britain

Contents

Introduction

A Baptism is always a very special and happy occasion. Usually it's the first 'formal' event in a child's life, and for the family it's a chance to get together and celebrate the new arrival. Of course, baby may cry all through the service, but that doesn't seem to stop everyone else enjoying the event!

Still, Baptism is a lot more than just a chance to say 'Welcome' to a new member of the human family. The service, as you will see, is about the child's relationship to God, and it only fulfils its real meaning when it's put in that setting. Your child is already a member of one family; now we welcome him or her into another – God's 'family', the family of the Church.

Most parents feel a great need to say 'thank you' to 'Someone, somewhere' for the wonderful gift of their child. Well, the 'Someone' is the God who gives life, and the 'somewhere' is the place where people gather to worship him. I do hope you enjoy the service.

David Winter

Planning for a Baptism

If you want to have your child baptized, the first step is to approach your vicar or minister. Baptisms normally take place in your parish church – that's to say, the parish where you live. The only exception is when the family is on the 'Electoral Roll' (membership list) of another parish. Baptisms almost always take place on a Sunday, often during one of the ordinary Sunday services, and you may find that there is a bit of a waiting list!

The vicar will tell you what preparation is required in your parish. This might mean one or two visits by the vicar, or by members of the congregation, or one or more meetings for parents. Sometimes you'll be invited to watch a video and certainly the service will be explained to you.

Godparents

At some point, an 'Application for Baptism' form will be filled in, and you'll be asked for the names of the proposed godparents. Usually a girl has two women and a man, and a boy two men and a woman – but that's a tradition, not a rule. There must be at least one godfather and one godmother, and at least one of the godparents must be a confirmed member of the Church. If you can't find one among your family or friends, the church will probably find one for you. As one promise is about bringing the child to confirmation, it makes sense for one godparent, at least, to be confirmed.

Choosing godparents is a serious business. Try to think of people who will do it well – who really will pray for the child and encourage him or her in their faith. Sometimes we tend to choose godparents because they're our friends, or because they asked us to do it in the past, or as potential guardians in case of something happening to us. But we ought also to ask, Will they take those promises seriously? Are they going to be in a position to help my child in his or her spiritual growth? Those are the really important tests.

Often you will find that the church has some members who take on a special concern for the children who are baptized there. They may deliver a card on the anniversary of the Baptism, or invite the child, as he or she grows older, to a toddler group or Sunday school. I hope you will recognize that this is done from the best of all motives: the good of your child. Both you and the Church have a responsibility for that once a baptism has taken place.

What to wear

In the past, children were often baptized in special christening robes, sometimes handed down through the generations. It's a lovely idea, but often modern children seem to grow rather faster than their predecessors. Nowadays it really doesn't matter what your child wears . . . and often children are baptized when they are three, four or five years old – and you won't get them into a christening robe!

Baptism – Then and Now

Baptism is a very ancient ceremony. The Jews were baptizing people long before the time of Jesus, and Jesus himself was baptized by John in the River Jordan. But Baptism as we know it – Christian Baptism – began with the first followers of Jesus. In obedience to his command, they 'baptized' people who wanted to follow him. They did it by pouring water over them, or dipping them in the water of a river, 'in the Name of the Father, the Son and the Holy Spirit' – the three 'Persons' of the Christian God.

Baptism was the sign that someone wanted to be a Christian, to join the Christian Church and follow Jesus Christ. People who were to be baptized had to 'repent' of their sins (that is, publicly turn from evil) and express their own belief in Jesus Christ. When they had done that, water was poured over them in the Name of the Trinity, and the mark of the cross was placed on their foreheads – usually with oil. This was a sign of belonging – a bit like marking a sheep with the brand of its owner. From that moment on, the baptized person was counted as a Christian believer and a member of the Church.

From the earliest times Baptism seems to have included the children of Christian believers. At least, whole households were baptized, and it's hard to believe they didn't sometimes include small children. Of course, the first converts to Christianity were adults, and so it was more common in those days for parents to be baptized – and their children with them.

Baptism is also known as 'christening' – an unofficial term which is still widely used. Originally it meant 'making Christian', but has come to be associated with the giving of a name. So most churches prefer the ancient and correct name of 'Baptism', which describes exactly what we do – 'wash' the candidate with water.

Baptism Today

All the main Christian Churches practise baptism, though Baptist churches restrict it to people old enough to make their own profession of faith. The Church of England and its sister Churches stand among the great majority who welcome children to baptism, provided their parents are willing to promise that they will be brought up within the Christian faith.

This is not just a matter of nominal assent. In the service, serious promises are made by parents and godparents – that they will pray for the child, encourage him or her in private prayer and public worship, and eventually to come to Confirmation, when a person takes on for themselves the promises made in their name at their Baptism.

Preparing for the Service

Most churches expect the parents to join in some simple preparation for the service, in which the obligations and promises that are going to be entered into are explained and discussed. Obviously, the Church doesn't want to encourage people to make promises they have no intention of keeping, so it's reasonable to make sure that everyone is clear about the meaning of this service. On the other hand, we know that Jesus welcomed the little children, and blessed them, so parents can be assured that no church wants to turn people away from God, especially children.

The promises made by the parents and godparents are made in their own name, and on behalf of the child. They are three: to 'turn to Christ', to 'repent of my sins' and to 'renounce evil'.

To 'turn to Christ' means to put our faith in him – to trust him with our lives.

To 'repent' means to turn away from all that has been wrong in our lives – to change the direction of our living.

To 'renounce evil' is to say that, recognizing what evil is, we want to have nothing to do with it in our lives.

As I've said, the promises are made by the parents and godparents in their own names, *and in the name of the child*. Our intention in this service, then, is that this child will put his or her life into Christ's hands, turn away from all that is evil and have nothing to do with it for the rest of their life.

Service of Thanksgiving

They are big, big promises, and you may not feel ready to make them yourself. In which case, most churches will offer you a simple service of 'Thanksgiving for the Birth of a Child' which will enable you to celebrate the new arrival without making promises and vows which you feel you may not be able to keep.

But most parents, wanting the best for their child, see the Baptism service as a lovely way of thanking God and introducing their child to a life of faith and goodness. If you come to it sincerely, even if you're 'new' to all these ideas, God will help you to give your child a good start on the journey of faith.

An opportunity for parents

Baptism isn't *just* for children, of course! Many adults are baptized nowadays as a sign that they wish to follow Christ. Sometimes one or both parents of a child take the opportunity of his or her baptism to make their own profession of faith and take their place within the Christian Church. If you have never been baptized, you might like to think about this, and discuss it with your minister.

The Baptism of Children

A Baptism service usually takes place around the font, which is often near the door at the back of the church. But sometimes the church has a 'portable' font which can be used at the front of the church, where everyone can see. In either case, the parents and godparents (and the child, of course!) will be invited to sit near it. The service begins with an explanation of the duties of parents and godparents – and of the church. For this, the parents and godparents stand, and are invited to say, out loud, that they are willing to take on the responsibility. If the child is old enough (say, over three) the minister may also explain to them what the service means – in very simple terms.

THE DUTIES OF PARENTS AND GODPARENTS

42 The priest says

Children who are too young to profess the Christian faith are baptized on the understanding that they are brought up as Christians within the family of the Church.

As they grow up, they need the help and encouragement of that family, so that they learn to be faithful in public worship and private prayer, to live by trust in God, and come to confirmation.

Parents and godparents, the *children* whom you have brought for baptism *depend* chiefly on you for the held and encouragement *they need*. Are you willing to give it to *them* by your prayers, by your example, and by your teaching?

Parents and godparents

I am willing.

43 And if the *child is* old enough to understand, the priest
speaks to *him* in these or similar words.

> *N*, when you are baptized, you become *a member* of a
> new family. God takes you for his own *child,* and all
> Christian people will be your brothers and sisters.

Sometimes at this point there will be an explanation, based on the
Bible, of the meaning of Baptism, after which the whole
congregation joins in a lovely prayer for the child who is to be
baptized.

THE MINISTRY OF THE WORD

Sections 44, 45, and 46 may be omitted when Baptism is
administered at Holy Communion or at Morning or Evening
Prayer.

44 Priest The Lord is loving to everyone;
All   and his mercy is over all his works.

45 Priest

God is the creator of all things, and by the birth of children he
gives to parents a share in the work and joy of creation. But we
who are born of earthly parents need to be born again. For in
the Gospel Jesus tells us that unless a man has been born again,
he cannot see the Kingdom of God. And so God gives us the
way to a second birth, a new creation and life in union with
him.

Baptism is the sign and seal of this new birth. In St Matthew's
Gospel we read of the risen Christ commanding his followers

to make disciples of all nations and to baptize men everywhere; and in the Acts of the Apostles we read of St Peter preaching in these words: Repent and be baptized in the name of Jesus Christ for the forgiveness of sins; and you shall receive the gift of the Holy Spirit. For the promise is to you and your children and to all that are afar off, everyone whom the Lord calls to him.

In obedience to this same command we ourselves were baptized and now bring *these children* to baptism.

46 Priest We thank God therefore for our baptism to life in Christ, and we pray for *these children (N)* and say together

All **Heavenly Father, in your love
you have called us to know you,
led us to trust you,
and bound our life with yours.
Surround** *these children* **with your love;
protect** *them* **from evil;
fill** *them* **with your Holy Spirit;
and receive** *them* **into the family of your Church;
that** *they* **may walk with us in the way of Christ
and grow in the knowledge of your love. Amen.**

Now the parents and godparents stand again, and are asked to make the three promises, 'for yourselves, and for this child'. Sometimes the 'signing with the cross' takes place here, but more often after the actual baptism.

THE DECISION

The parents and godparents stand, and the priest says to them

Those who bring children to be baptized must affirm their allegiance to Christ and their rejection of all that is evil.

It is your duty to bring up *these children* to fight against evil and to follow Christ.

48   Therefore I ask these questions which you must answer for yourselves and for *these children*.

Do you turn to Christ?
Answer   **I turn to Christ.**

Do you repent of your sins?
Answer   **I repent of my sins.**

Do you renounce evil?
Answer   **I renounce evil.**

Either here or at section 56 the priest makes THE SIGN OF THE CROSS on the forehead of each child, saying to each

I sign you with the cross, the sign of Christ.

After the signing of each or all, he says

Do not be ashamed to confess the faith of Christ crucified.

All   **Fight valiantly under the banner of Christ against sin, the world, and the devil, and continue his faithful** *soldiers* **and** *servants* **to the end of your** *lives.*

50   Priest   May almighty God deliver you from the powers of darkness, and lead you in the light and obedience of Christ. **Amen.**

Now the water which is to be used for the Baptism is 'blessed' –
that's to say, we give thanks for the gift of water and set this
particular water aside for the purpose of Christian baptism.

THE BAPTISM

52   The priest stands before the water of baptism and says

> Praise God who made heaven and earth,
> **All   who keeps his promise for ever.**

Priest   Almighty God, whose Son Jesus Christ
　　　　was baptized in the river Jordan:
　　　we thank you for the gift of water
　　　　to cleanse us and revive us;
　　　we thank you that through the waters of the
　　　　Red Sea, you led your people out of slavery
　　　　to freedom in the promised land;
　　　we thank you that through the deep waters
　　　　of death you brought your Son, and raised
　　　　him to life in triumph.
　　　Bless this water, that your *servants* who *are*
　　　　washed in it may be made one with Christ in his
　　　　death and in his resurrection,
　　　　to be cleansed and delivered from all sin.
　　　Send your Holy Spirit upon *them* to bring
　　　　them to new birth in the family of your
　　　　Church, and raise *them* with Christ
　　　　to full and eternal life.
　　　For all might, majesty, authority, and power
　　　　are yours, now and for ever. **Amen.**

The parents and godparents – still standing – are now asked to affirm the three basic statements of the Christian faith – belief in God as Father, Son and Spirit. 'Believe and trust' is not saying the same thing twice! We 'believe' with our reason and we 'trust' with our hearts!

53 The priest says to the parents and godparents

You have brought *these children* to baptism. You must now declare before God and his Church the Christian faith into which *they are* to be baptized, and in which you will help *them* to grow. You must answer for yourselves and for *these children*.

Do you believe and trust in God the Father,
who made the world?

Answer   **I believe and trust in him.**

Do you believe and trust in his Son Jesus Christ,
who redeemed mankind?

Answer   **I believe and trust in him.**

Do you believe and trust in his Holy Spirit,
who gives life to the people of God?

Answer   **I believe and trust in him.**

54 The priest turns to the congregation and says

This is the faith of the Church.
All   This is our faith.
We believe and trust in one God,
Father, Son, and Holy Spirit.

The minister will take the child into his arms, and usually asks the parents to 'name this child'. What is required is their 'Christian' names – all of them! Then the child is baptized by name, with the water being poured over their head – it's usually warm water! Then the sign of the cross is made, and the whole congregation joins in the traditional words.

---

55 The parents and godparents being present with each child, the priest baptizes *him*. He dips *him* in the water or pours water on *him*, addressing *him* by name.

> *N*, I baptize you in the name of the Father, and of the Son, and of the Holy Spirit.

And each one of *his* sponsors answers

> **Amen.**

56 The priest makes THE SIGN OF THE CROSS on the forehead of each child if he has not already done so. The appropriate words are printed at section 19.

Often nowadays the child (or a parent) is given a lighted candle – a very ancient baptismal tradition – a sign of light conquering darkness as Christ conquered evil.

Baptism is a service based on promises: God's promise to us, that through Jesus we can be forgiven, accepted and welcomed into his family; and our promise to him, that we will turn from evil and put our trust in his Son, Jesus. Perhaps the baptism candle, kept at home and lit on Sundays, birthdays or other occasions, may help to remind us both of God's promises (which he always keeps) and of ours, which we probably need his help in keeping!

---

57 The priest or other person may give to a parent or godparent for each child A LIGHTED CANDLE, saying to each

>Receive this light.

And when a candle has been given to each one, he says

>This is to show that you have passed
>from darkness to light.

All **Shine as a light in the world**
to the glory of God the Father.

Finally, the child is welcomed – by the whole congregation . . . a fitting climax to a service which is all about God's welcome to us. And then we pray, often using on this family occasion the words of the 'family' prayer, 'Our Father'.

THE WELCOME

58 The priest and the congregation, representing the whole Church, welcome the newly baptized.

Priest God has received you by baptism into his Church.
All **We welcome you into the Lord's Family.**
We are members together of the body of Christ;
we are children of the same heavenly Father;
we are inheritors together of the kingdom
of God.
We welcome you.

THE PRAYERS

59 The prayers that follow are omitted when Baptism is administered at Holy Communion; and may be omitted when Baptism is administered at Morning or Evening Prayer.

Priest Lord God our Father, maker of heaven and earth, we
thank you that by your Holy Spirit *these children have*
been born again into new life, adopted for your own,
and received into the fellowship of your Church:
grant that *they* may grow in the faith
into which *they have* been baptized,
that *they* may profess it for *themselves*
when *they come* to be confirmed,
and that all things belonging to the Spirit
may live and grow in *them*. **Amen.**

60 Priest Heavenly Father, we pray for the parents of *these
children;* give them the spirit of wisdom and love, that
their *homes* may reflect the joy of your eternal kingdom.
Amen.

61 Priest Almighty God, we thank you for our fellowship in the
household of faith with all those who have been baptized
in your name. Keep us faithful to our baptism, and so
make us ready for that day when the whole creation
shall be made perfect in your Son, our Saviour Jesus
Christ. **Amen.**

62 Priest Jesus taught us to call God our Father, and so in
faith and trust we say

All **Our Father in heaven,
hallowed be your name,
your kingdom come,
your will be done,
on earth as in heaven.
Give us today our daily bread.
Forgive us our sins**

as we forgive those who sin against us.
Lead us not into temptation
but deliver us from evil.

For the kingdom, the power, and the glory
    are yours
now and for ever. Amen

63 Priest The grace of our Lord Jesus Christ, and the love of God,
and the fellowship of the Holy Spirit be with us all
evermore. **Amen.**

Part of a new family

At the end of the baptism service we welcome the child into 'the Lord's family'. In other words, he or she is now a member of the Christian Church – a 'child of the same heavenly Father' as all other Christians.

When we are born we automatically become members of a family. We don't choose it, and it may be very small – even, just two people! But it's our family and we belong to it.

Becoming a Christian is likened in the Bible to being 'born again'. And in this birth, too, we join a new family – the family of all those others who also believe in Jesus Christ. From now on we 'belong' with them.

So it's only natural that those who have been baptized should want to express that 'belonging' by taking their full part in the life of the Church – certainly joining in worship Sunday by Sunday, but also trying to grow in their faith. Many people find that the friendship and fellowship of the church is a great source of strength to them.

This is as true for children as for adults! In their baptism it's as though we've planted a seed of faith in their lives. But to grow into a strong plant that seed is going to need nourishment and support. We can provide that at home, by praying with our child and reading them stories from the Bible.

We can help by taking them to church with us, and showing them that we value what we can learn there. And we can help by teaching them things like the Lord's Prayer, and the Ten Commandments.

Faith, for most of us, is a process rather than a crisis, and Baptism is a starting point for that process. If we see it in that way, we shall be able to help our child to discover, bit by bit, the wonderful purpose God has for their life, and to know the security and peace that comes from faith in a loving and reliable God.

The Lord's Prayer

Jesus gave us his own prayer to pray. Here is the traditional version together with one written in simple language for young children.

> *Our Father*
> *who art in heaven,*
> *hallowed be thy name;*
> *thy kingdom come;*
> *thy will be done;*
> *on earth as it is in heaven.*
> *Give us this day our daily bread.*
> *And forgive us our trespasses,*
> *as we forgive those who trespass against us.*
> *And lead us not into temptation;*
> *but deliver us from evil.*
> *For thine is the kingdom, the power, and the glory,*
> *for ever and ever.*
> *Amen.*

> *Our Father in heaven:*
> *Your name is very special to us.*
> *Be king of our hearts*
> *so that we do what you want on earth*
> *as they do in heaven.*
> *Give us today the food we need.*
> *Forgive us when we do wrong things,*
> *and help us to forgive those who are unkind to us.*
> *Please stop us from doing bad things,*
> *and keep us safe from every danger.*
> *Our hearts are yours.*
> *You have all the power*
> *and all the glory,*
> *for ever and ever.*
> *Amen.*

The Ten Commandments

Here are the ten commandments from the Old Testament book of Exodus chapter 20, together with a version in simple language for young children.

God spoke all these words, saying, I am the Lord your God, who brought you out of the land of Egypt . . .
You shall have no other gods before me.
You shall not make for yourself graven images . . . you shall not bow down to them or serve them . . .
You shall not take the name of the Lord your God in vain.
Remember the sabbath day, to keep it holy.
Honour your father and your mother.
You shall not kill.
You shall not commit adultery.
You shall not steal.
You shall not bear false witness against your neighbour.
You shall not covet anything that is your neighbour's.

I am God. I have always taken care of my people. You must love and obey me only.
Don't let anything be more important than me.
You must respect me, and take care how you speak about me.
Keep my day of rest, one special day each week.
Show respect to your mother and father.
Do not kill.
Husbands and wives: keep your special love just for each other.
Do not steal.
Do not tell lies.
Do not be greedy for the things other people have.

Prayers

God our Father, maker of all that is living, we praise you for the wonder and joy of creation. We thank you from our hearts for the life of this child, for a safe delivery, and for the privilege of parenthood. Accept our thanks and praise through Jesus Christ our Lord.

FROM THE ALTERNATIVE SERVICE BOOK 1980

This is ....
We thank God for him/her.
We offer him/her back to God.
We pray for him/her and all his/her family.
We welcome him/her into this family of believers.

Father, we thank you that you have given us families so that we can grow up surrounded by love. Thank you, too that we belong to the wider family of your church, surrounding us with those who love and serve you.

Lord Jesus Christ, we come to you with our baby, we give this new life into your care. As weakness turns into maturity, may our child grow to love and trust you. Lord Jesus, draw us together in deeper love and understanding so that our child may grow up in security and peace.

CHRISTIAN PUBLICITY ORGANIZATION

Other books from Lion Publishing

The Lord's Prayer for Children by Lois Rock

The Ten Commandments for Children by Lois Rock

The Little Lion Prayer Collection:
Everyday Prayers
Everyday Graces
Goodnight Prayers
Prayers for Special Days

My Little Book of Prayers by Felicity Henderson

Jigsaw Prayer Books by Lois Rock
Hooray for the World
My Special Friend

My Own Book of Prayers by Mary Batchelor

My Own Book of Bible Stories by Pat Alexander

The Best for Your Child by David and Christine Winter